Would You Rather?

Copyright Protected. All rights reserved. ™
No part of this publication may be reproduced, stored, copied or shared by any means, electronic or physical, or used in any manner without the prior written consent of the publisher.

HOW TO PLAY

This couples Do You know Me Game? is a "Would You Rather...?" Game with a twist!

It's a fun guessing game to discover how well you know each other; what makes you happy? what you value? and what's really important to you?

(If you find you don't know each other that well, in the process of playing the game together you will remedy that! You will deepen your connection and ignite your intimacy!)

1. Decide on how many questions you want to answer for each game each time you play, for example let's say 20 questions.
2. Multiply the number of questions you picked X2. This gives you the number of points you both have (in the example above you would have 40 points each).
3. Partner 1 asks a question out loud and tries to guess what partner 2's answer would be within 10 seconds and has to give a reason why they think partner 2 would choose that option. Partner 2 then reveals their truth - what option they would actually pick and the main reason for it.
    - If partner 1 chooses the right option with the valid reason then they don't lose any points
    - If partner 1 chooses the right option but with an invalid reason then they lose 1 point.
    - If partner 1 chooses the wrong option then they lose 2 points
    - If the time runs out and partner 1 just can't decide then they also lose 2 points.

4. Take turns asking the questions and tracking points.
5. Keep asking the questions till you get to the end of the questions.
6. The partner with the most points remaining wins and is crowned the BETTER HALF! in the relationship. 😊

This game is not only a fun activity but a great way to introduce play and novelty into your relationship to help it soar to new heights!

This game will allow you to discover what your partner thinks really makes you happy and this will help explain why they behave the way they do towards you (most of us really do want to please each other if we know how).

Please remember if they get some answers wildly wrong (and are losing points like they are going out of style), to view it as a great opportunity to educate them and look forward to how amazing your relationship can be from now on as they now know better!

Optional Tip: you can also use the book to get to know each other better as fun "conversation starters" by taking time to discuss why each person would make their choice without competing for points.

Have fun!

Would you rather a date at a fancy expensive restaurant

or

a date having street food at a amusement park?

Would you rather have loved and lost

or

never have loved at all?

Would you rather your partner have an emotional affair

or

physically cheat on you?

Would you rather have 5 children

or

no children?

Would you rather have an indoor wedding at a castle

or

an outdoor wedding on a hot beach?

Would you rather spend your life with someone you don't love but they love you

or

someone who doesn't love you but you love them?

Would you rather be with someone who loves/admires themselves a bit too much

or

someone who has too little self-esteem?

Would you rather be with a partner who primarily makes decisions using their head

or

their heart?

Would you rather be a psychopath

or

mentally retarded?

Would you rather have a needy partner who is too clingy

or

someone who emotionally neglects you?

Would you rather (on a third date) do a stinky poo at your date's home and the smell travels out the bathroom

or

burp in their face when they try to kiss you?

Would you rather your partner has lots of friends of the opposite gender

or

no friends?

Would you rather experience love at first sight

or

fall in love with someone over 1-2 years?

Would you rather make your partner laugh

or

turn them on?

Would you rather your partner was more religious

or

more helpful around the house?

Would you rather receive a small meaningful gift from your partner

or

a less meaningful expensive gift?

Would you rather a date movie night

or

a long romantic walk?

Would you rather break another person's heart

or

let someone break your heart?

Would you rather move in with your partner before you get married

or

only after you get married?

Would you rather your partner was always overdressed at events

or

always underdressed?

Would you rather be a tutor for underprivileged kids

or

volunteer at a homeless shelter?

Would you rather sext all day with your partner

or

send loving messages all day?

Would you rather be a genius

or

look the way you've always wanted to?

Would you rather your partner liked to make you laugh mentally

or

was physically playful with you like pillow fights, tickles etc?

Would you rather tell everyone your guilty pleasures

or

never be able to experience any of your guilty pleasures ever again?

Would you rather have a personal chef

or

a personal financial advisor?

Would you rather tell a white lie if the situation only affects you

or

always tell the truth no matter what?

Would you rather stay in

or

go out for a date?

Would you rather be able to be invisible

or

have the power of moving things with your mind?

Would you rather your partner was too romantic (so it sometimes makes you feel cringe)

or

not romantic enough?

Would you rather right now have a pet

or

a child?

Would you rather never have to shave/get rid of unwanted hair again

or

never have to brush your teeth?

Would you rather experience numerous short, passionate love affairs in your life

or

one long-term relationship with less passion and more comfort?

Would you rather tell your partner you love them in person

or

via text?

Would you rather be with someone who doesn't love you but they are faithful

or

someone who does love you but they cheat?

Would you rather spend $5000 on clothes

or

homeware?

Would you rather have a partner who is never jealous

or

jealous too much?

Would you rather when you're old be physically healthy but declining mentally

or

mentally healthy and declining physically?

Would you rather cuddle and spoon your partner all night

or

make out all night?

Would you rather follow your head

or

your heart when making big decisions about your love life?

Would you rather be ghosted

or

get dumped during a phone call where the person explains why you are not right for them?

Would you rather be loved

or

respected by your partner?

Would you rather be a bird

or

a lion?

Would you rather let your partner check your text messages

or

read your diary?

Would you rather experience what it's like to be 16 again

or

21?

Would you rather send a loving text in the morning

or

at night?

Would you rather slow dance with your partner

or

go clubbing with your partner?

Would you rather give up kissing

or

give up sex?

Would you rather meet a famous celebrity you admire

or

a significant historical figure?

Would you rather lose all of your photos ever taken with your partner

or

lose every gift they've ever given you?

Would you rather be with a partner who never argues with you

or

who never cuddles you?

Would you rather be with a partner who likes to dress fashionably

or

dress comfortably?

Would you rather your parents together but miserable

or

divorced and happy?

Would you rather have a rich but dumb partner

or

poor but smart partner?

Would you rather be an incredible artist

or

incredible musician?

Would you rather spend your last moments with family

or

doing something adventurous you've alway wanted to do?

Would you rather be your favorite superhero for a year

or

your favorite celebrity?

Would you rather drink as much as you want to without ever getting drunk

or

eat as much as you want to without ever getting fat?

Would you rather work for your partner and so see them a lot (but you're both in work mode)

or

not work with them and see them mainly on the weekends?

Would you rather listen to a new song that you love

or

watch a new movie that you love?

Would you rather spend a year in prison as a prisoner

or

a year in a hospital, as a patient?

Would you rather skydive

or

scuba dive?

Would you rather be with someone smarter then you

or

better looking then you?

Would you rather celebrate Christmas day

or

your anniversary with your partner?

Would you rather know how to dance salsa

or

ballroom dance?

Would you rather be in a relationship with someone who is 10 years younger than you

or

someone who is 10 years older?

Would you rather read a book with your partner

or

watch a movie with your partner?

Would you rather be desired by lots of people (but your partner only half desires you)

or

not be desired by anyone but your partner and they really deeply desire you?

Would you rather accidentally upload an embarrassing video of yourself to the internet and it goes viral

or

upload an embarrassing video of a loved one?

Would you rather have an arranged marriage

or

never get married?

Would you rather get passionately kissed at your work place

or

trip and fall at your workplace?

Would you rather give up eating your favorite food for

5 years

or

social media for 1 year?

Would you rather your partner shows you they love you by their actions but hardly says it

or

tells you they love you a lot but does little to show it via their actions?

Would you rather be someone who is very smart but has few friends

or

kinda dumb but has many friends?

Would you rather be a rich celebrity whose always hounded by paparazzi when you go outside

or

be as you are now and not get bothered?

Would you rather be with a partner who has different political views then you

or

different interests then you?

Would you rather lose your arms

or

your legs?

Would you rather give up your favorite thing to do (outside of spending time with your partner) for 3 months

or

not be able to see your partner for 3 months?

Would you rather be able to speak to animals

or

be able to read other's minds?

Would you rather your partner had a job that was life threatening but you get to see them a lot

or

safe but you only get to see them on the weekends?

Would you rather have a personal masseuse

or

housekeeper?

Would you rather your partner cook you a special meal

or

take you out to a special restaurant?

Would you rather have an amazing wedding day

or

an amazing honeymoon?

Would you rather be a parent at 18

or

never get to be a parent?

Would you rather your partner sing you a love song

or

do a flashdance for you?

Would you rather be with a partner who is sometimes too competitive with you

or

sometimes too coddling and smothering?

Would you rather have the ability to freeze time

or

move objects with your mind?

Would you rather your partner always wants to hold your hand when you go out

or

doesn't like any public displays of affection?

Would you rather die in 20 years with no regrets

or

40 years with lots of regrets?

Would you rather lose the ability to read

or

lose the ability to speak?

Would you rather spend $10,000 on traveling

or

on physical items?

Would you rather do karaoke with your partner

or

climb a mountain?

Would you rather cure cancer but never get to fall in love

or

fall in love and not cure cancer?

Would you rather no one showed up at your funeral

or

no one showed up at your wedding?

Would you rather abstain from sex for one year

or

take a vow of silence?

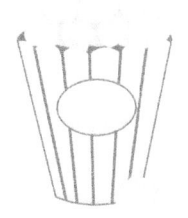

Would you rather watch a good movie alone

or

a bad movie with your partner?

Would you rather be proposed to in a public

or

private place?

Would you rather never be able to eat meat again

or

never be able to eat desert again?

Would you rather be respected by your parents

or

your friends?

Would you rather your partner compliment you so much it sometimes gets on your nerves

or

too little so you are unsure if they really appreciate you?

Would you rather never watch TV again

or

never use social media again?

Would you rather be a successful celebrity

or

a successful politician?

Would you rather be able to control technology with your mind

or

animals with your mind?

Would you rather be able to change one physical thing about you now

or

change one significant thing about your career right now?

Would you rather have a partner whose very ambitious

or

very kind?

Would you rather be relatively rich living in a small boring town

or

relatively poor living in a big exciting city?

Would you rather your next holiday be a relaxing one in a hot country

or

activity based one in a cold country?

Would you rather your partner is not a big hugger

or

not a big kisser?

Would you rather your partner (who you love very much) liked to dress up in your clothes and doesn't tell you

or

does tell you?

Would you rather be able to go back and change one significant thing in your life

or

go into the future and change one significant thing?

Would you rather your partner sulks and gives you the silent treatment after an argument

or

says rude things they don't mean during an argument but then doesn't sulk after?

Would you rather work in a job you hate for 10 years that's paid well so you can retire after that

or

work a job you enjoy for 30 more years?

Would you rather receive a love letter

or

a curated playlist of love songs especially for you?

Would you rather get a foot rub

or

head massage?

Would you rather be able to have access to your partner's social media for one day

or

their email account?

Would you rather be with someone who likes to talk about their feelings a lot (and it sometimes feels like too much)

or

someone who prefers not to (but you sometimes feel like you don't know them)?

Would you rather your partner was still friends with their ex's

or

not friends with any of them?

Would you rather take a road trip with your partner

or

stay at a luxury resort?

Would you rather have an amazing morning

or

an amazing night?

Would you rather have parents who embarrass you

or

parents who claim you embarrass them?

Would you rather you were an extrovert

or

an introvert?

Would you rather your partner likes to go shopping with you

or

likes to do a physical acitivity with you?

Would you rather live in the best house in a bad neighbourhood

or

the worst house in a good neighbourhood?

Would you rather love the sound of your partner's voice

or

the way they smell?

Would you rather be with a partner with a 'live for the now' kind of attitude

or

who likes to plan for the future?

Would you rather be funny

or

be able to sing really well?

Would you rather your partner's love language is different then what it is

or

yours is different then what it is?

Would you rather be with someone whose very fit (but it sometimes makes you feel intimidated/accountable)

or

someone whose not as fit as you'd like?

Would you rather tell your partner about your fantasies

or

have your partner tell you about their fantasies?

Would you rather learn to ski

or

learn to surf?

Would you rather send a revealing flirty photo to your partner

or

receive one from them?

Would you rather your partner was more into science and technology

or

more artistic?

Would you rather spend more time with your partner but have less money

or

have more money and a better lifestyle but less time?

Would you rather your partner liked to whisper sweet words into your ear more

or

that you were better at doing it to them?

Would you rather your partner snores so it wakes you up at night

or

doesn't snore but likes to go to bed later then you so you don't get to fall asleep together?

Perfect Pair

Would you rather your partner can't dance but tries for you

or

can dance, but doesn't enjoy it so doesn't dance with you much?

Would you rather be known as someone who knows how to dress really well

or

someone whose very friendly?

Would you rather your partner give you a massage before sex

or

pamper you for the night by cleaning the house and making dinner for you (when it's your turn) before sex?

Would you rather your partner loves to be the centre of attention

or

prefers to be more of an observer and listener?

Would you rather get to meet and spend one day with your partner when they were a child

or

when they are 90?

Hope you had lots of fun!

Now go have some more...

Made in the USA
Las Vegas, NV
05 November 2023